A limerick romp through time

Arnie Wilson

TSL Publications

First published in Great Britain in 2017
By TSL Publications, Rickmansworth

ISBN / 978-1-911070-75-7

Grateful thanks to *Express Newspapers* for permission to include limericks pre-
viously published. These are marked with asterisks.

About Arnie Wilson

Although Arnie Wilson comes from an artistic background (his father, Bernard, was a composer who met his wife Joan, a concert pianist, at London's Wigmore Hall where they were both featured in a concert) he has inherited few of their talents. "I failed to learn the French horn, my favourite instrument, but did manage to play the flute in the Canterbury Youth Orchestra for a while," he says. It was as a journalist rather than as a flautist that Wilson made his mark. He spent 15 years in television – on screen for 10 of them – and several years in Fleet Street, before becoming the *Financial Times* ski correspondent and skiing every day of the year in 1994 (thus entering the *Guinness Book of Records*). He also wrote regularly for the *FT*, occasionally interviewing celebrities for the paper's "Lunch With The FT" feature. Between 2001 and 2013 he edited *Ski+board*, the Ski Club of Great Britain's magazine. Wilson, who has four skiing daughters from his first marriage, is the author of several books, most of them about skiing. He and his Swedish wife, Vivianne – who were married on the mountain at Jackson Hole, Wyoming in 2000 – live in West Sussex, England.

To my daughters Melissa, Samantha, Amber and Lara
and my wife Vivianne
who sometimes asks which planet I'm on.
For my part I'm convinced it's she who's from
another planet.

Said Vivi "I've come from afar
Much too distant to get here by car
The journey was lonely
But I love Arnie only
So I won't miss my home on North Star"

CONTENTS

Peter James

(international best-selling writer of crime fiction)

Foreword

As someone who specialises in mysteries of all kinds and at all levels, it remains something of a mystery even to me how my old friend Arnie Wilson manages to write such daft but undeniably amusing limericks. In fact they're Dead Funny! (Regular readers of my Roy Grace thrillers will get that pun-ishing joke.)

I've tried to emulate his limerick-writing skills, but I barely make the championship to his premiership. Luckily for me, he can't write thrillers – at last I don't think he can. Put it this way: I haven't seen his name in the best-sellers' fiction list. So my career seems safe from any Arnie competition in the thriller market – for the time being at least. Can you imagine what would happen if he did have a go at a Detective Superintendent Roy Grace novel? It might start something like this:

It's a completely mysterious case –
A murder, a villain, a chase ...
Only one boy in blue
Could solve every clue
And that of course, is Roy Grace!

No. I don't think that's going to grip his readers. Do you?

I've known Arnie for more than 20 years and for some unknown reason we're still fond of each other. They say that a true friend is someone who knows everything about you and still likes you. Guess that's true of us. We have, I think, a similar sense of humour – (though his is not as dark as mine!). And we also like to indulge in that strangely British habit of affectionately insulting each other. Which is why he likes to be rude to me, the swine, in some of his limericks. Such as:

When a Charterhouse reject called Pete
Found it terribly hard to complete
His latest Roy Grace
He gave up the race –
Joined the Met, where he's pounding the beat

How cruel! And how untrue! But that's "friendship" for you!

You'll notice quite a few of his limericks are about skiing. That's because Arnie's quite a good skier. He should be because he was the *Financial Times* ski correspondent for 15 years and went on to edit the Ski Club of Great Britain's magazine, *Ski+board* for 13 years. As someone who was on the fringe of the English ski team myself, I like to think I can ski him off the mountain – any mountain. We always have a joke about "proper" old fashioned long "skinny" skis which you had to be a fairly good skier to turn, and more modern and shorter "carving" skis which make turning so much easier. In fact it could be said that carving skis virtu- ally turn themselves. When carving skis first came in around the turn of the century (the trend started earlier in fact – in the mid-1990s) I teased him about using them (although of course I secretly liked them too) – which may just be why he so cruelly and churlishly wrote this:

Said my snooty mate Pete with a wheeze
"Me try carvers? They'd ruin my knees."
"Short skis are for dames"
Said the vain Mr James
And promptly fell over his skis

So why are we still friends? It's a bit of a mystery! And maybe we won't be after he reads this:
Arnie kept all his cronies in fits
As he churned out his daft limericks
They never rhymed; rarely scanned
And were frequently panned
Were they funny? Well, only in bits!

Only kidding of course. I have to (reluctantly) admit that Arnie does write some very entertaining limericks, as you'll see in the following pages. But only if HE finally admits that I'm a better skier than he is!

Introduction

Limericks. You can view them as silly, irrelevant and infantile nonsense. Or as witty, nicely balanced and subtle jokes. For me it all depends on the punchline. And yet when the father of limericks, Edward Lear, made them so popular in the 19th century the established custom was that the last line was often essentially a repeat of the first line. To me this is all wrong. A bit of a damp squib in fact. An anti-climax.

I believe the last line should provide, when possible, an unexpected explosion – or at least a pleasant chuckle – of mirth. For this reason I usually write the last line first so that the joke is taken care of. And then work backwards. I'm also a great believer in limericks that scan. This can be tricky as sometimes a word or syllable can be pronounced or emphasised in different ways, so depending on how you pronounce it, it can make a line scan – or fail to scan.

Here's an example, based on a genuine screening of *Spectre* I went to in Innsbruck in 2015.

We all viewed the latest James Bond
Of whom we are all very fond
But what WAS it about?
All the words were in Kraut!
Overall we were jolly well conned!

Unless you stress the word WAS by putting it in block capitals, and just say what was it about, it suddenly doesn't scan.

Sometimes, just for fun, you can deliberately make a limerick scan so badly and not even rhyme that this in itself can be funny. I was prompted to put this book together when a friend, Steve Hartridge bought me a book of limericks by Michael Palin for my birthday recently. Which prompted the following:

On receiving a book of fine verse
Arnie struggled and stumbled and cursed
He wanted to pen
A limerick but then
He couldn't think of any words that rhymed with Limerick!

I discovered I apparently had a flare for limericks when I was working for Peter Tory, a prominent and witty Fleet Street daily paper columnist who decided one day that it would be fun to include a weekly verse from a book of limericks we happened to have in the office. After we'd done this for a few weeks, I thought it might be fun to write one for him myself, not really expecting him to use it. But he liked it so much that he did use it, and thereafter, for a year or two, I wrote a weekly limerick for him, often based on a major news story that had happened that week. This continued when Peter and I switched to running a Sunday column, so the "Friday Limerick" became the "Sunday Limerick".

Although they are no longer published in Fleet Street, I love writing limericks for friends, and they seem to enjoy receiving them. It's something quite personal for them, I suppose, whereas the idea of writing an ordinary poem for your friends would seem a little – shall we say – cringe-worthy. So you could say that limericks do have something of a purpose. In a funny way!

Thanks to the late Peter Tory's encouragement, who used almost 100 of my limericks in his Diary columns in the *Star* and *The Sunday Express* in the '80s and early '90s, I seem to be addicted to writing limericks. Or trying to. As often as not for friends. I do think a book of them might make good stocking fillers.

Unlike Edward Lear's, the last line of my limericks is NOT a repeat of the first line and the last line also usually contains a (hopefully) funny pay off. What's more – my limericks do usually scan! Listen to me blowing my own trumpet! Peter Tory was for a while a spear-carrier with the Royal Shakespeare Company. On tour in *King Lear*, he was always tempted to change the words of the one line he had: "Edmund is dead, My Lord." What he'd have loved to say was: "Edmund is sitting up and taking notice, my Lord!" Hence the following:

An ode to Peter Tory on his 50th birthday
"I'm 50" said Tory, "and bored.
"I shall go back to acting" he roared.
His comeback went fine
Till he fluffed his one line
Saying: "Edmund is better my Lord."

On the art of writing limericks ...
When writing those five lines of verse
Many limerick writers are cursed
When their search for great wit
Lacks the most vital bit
Solved by writing the last sentence first.

A limerick writer called Hayes
Kept falling asleep in mid-phrase
He'd be doing just fine
Till the very last line
And then zzzzzzzz

A not particularly gifted poet from Oman
Wrote limericks that didn't scan
All he knew about meter
Was that it was some foreign measurement a bit like litre
And the last line was usually worse than when he began

Here's one about Peter Tory's brilliant secretary-cum-office-manager:
One could always tell with Jeanette
When she thought that a freelance was wet
She would spill lukewarm tea
All over his knee
And glare if he dare be upset

And one more credit: I have to thank Keith Howard, Membership Secretary of the Eagle Society for this book being published (it's a long story). But when I met Keith I was with my cartoonist friend Neil Linnert who drew the cover page of this book. And even he was inspired to write a limerick to celebrate! (See how catching they are?)
I nearly fell out of my chair,
When you told me that out of thin air,
When out with pal Neil
You were offered a deal.
Which all started thanks to Dan Dare!

***

As we were preparing to go to press, news came in that the Duchess of Cornwall was a fan of Peter's books. This prompted me to write:

When a Peter James fan called Camilla
Took for ever to read his new thriller
Prince Charles, in a rage
Tore out the last page
Now she's just no idea who's the killer!

Showbiz/Celebs

Luckily I can insult my closest friends, including the best-selling thriller writer Peter James!
　When Pete asked the top glitterati
　To his ever-so-posh birthday party
　One by one the old tossers
　Said they'd had better offers
　Each one much more trendy and arty

Peter once wrote a great Guardian *feature about Shakespeare:*
　Said Peter: "I love Shakespeare madly
　And the murder scenarios (sadly!)
　I too write about death –
　Could have written Macbeth!
　I'm afraid that all's well can end badly."

Peter James has used the word Dead *in all 13 of his Roy Grace thriller titles – from* Dead Simple *to* Need You Dead. *Will he ever run out of titles?*
　Dead Worrying!
　Unable to sleep in his bed
　Peter James sighed and groaned as he said:
　"Though It's utterly vital
　For my next Roy Grace title ...
　I've used all the ones that say... Dead"

My friend, Tony Coe, one of the world's greatest saxophon-ists who played on the sound track of the Pink Panther *movies and* Superman 2.

A saxophone player called Coe
Played wonderful jazz, high and low
He'd play on his horn
From dusk until dawn
And ravers would not let him go!

On a 1990 expedition to Botswana with my old friend Col. John Blashford-Snell
"We're lost" said Big John from his car
"My Magellan's not showing one star
I'm afraid that without it
There's no doubt about it
I don't know my AH! From my HA!"

For Greta Scacchi (presented to her at Jeremy's, my favour-ite restaurant). No fire without smoke?
At a poetry reading, Miss Scacchi
Packed a punch like a tumbler of sake
Was that magical voice
(Like a purring Rolls Royce)
Enhanced by a quick drag of baccy?

To which she gamely replied (introducing skiing as I'd asked her if she ever went) – and even signed off her limerick.
So glad you enjoyed the show
No, not much of a skier, but I'll go
For the sake of the kids
And attempt a few skis
'Cos there's nothing they like more than snow
(See ya, Gret!)

In praise of Fowler's Dictionary of Modern Usage
   There was an old chappie called Fowler
   Who trained as a literary prowler
   He spent all his days
   Checking out every phrase
   Saying "there goes another big howler!"

More on Fowler
   When a silly old git and his Fowler,
   Thought his girl had committed a howler.
   He snarled and he swore
   And regardless of gore
   He threatened to just disembowel'er

My friend James Bedding forgave me for this (I think!)
   A young travel writer called Bedding
   Was a guest at an African wedding
   But his plans came to nowt
   And it later turned out
   That he'd never been further than Reading

*Sir Geoffrey, live from Big Ben
   Said: "They've cocked up my pension again –
   Can you spare 50p
   For a hot cup of tea ...?
   Geoffrey Cox, down and out, News at Ten."
(former chief exec of ITN and founder of News at Ten)

The great TV front-man, Alastair Burnet
   *A trouserless newsman went spare
   When his fans saw his kneecaps on air
   He looked such a sight
   As he yelped out: "Goodnight ...
   Al Burnet, Nude at Ten, almost bare!"

18

*Their agent said "Listen you guys –
Eric's real name we'll have to disguise ...
This Bartholomew thing
Doesn't have a good ring.
Let's agree – you'll be Morecambe and Wise."

*When Janet Street Porter was tipped to take over the BBC's
culture programmes:*
*"My cultural plans" said Miss Porter
"Are to cut La Boheme by a quart'a
We'll get Brahms and Liszt an'
Get Cliff to sing Tristan
Then film Wagner's Ring under wort'a!"

This one's about the late great Sir Terry Wogan:
*Said Terry "I know what to do
Now I've eased up on Radio 2
My next major mission?
My lifelong ambition?
To be cast as the next Doctor Who!"

*It must be the dream of every red-blooded male to run out of
fuel on a country road with Joanna Lumley in the passenger
seat ...*

*But, far from being embarrassed, she leapt out of the car
and helped me push it to the nearest garage (downhill, it
should be stressed).*
"Joanna!" I yelled, changing gear,
"We've run out of petrol I fear!"
She said "That's not fab
But don't hail a cab –
I'll get out and push, Arnie dear!"

Sports

Said a skier called Einstein: "I'm weary
Of skiing so fast that quite clearly
When I ski at such height
I must *schuss* fast as light –
But I must say it's only a theory ...!"

Mike Browne is the founder of Snow+Rock *mountain equip-
ment chain.*
A skier called Mike had a titfer
That all kinds of weather were fit fer
In fact there was no
Variety of snow
That he didn't have adequate kit fer

*My friend Andy Perrin, Chairman of the Hotelplan UK
group of travel companies.*
A handsome young fisherman, Perrin
Was never forthcoming at sharin'
His diminutive catch ...
But pr'aps that was natch
As he rarely caught more than a herrin'

My much-missed old friend the late Nigel Lloyd.
An entire Swiss resort was destroyed
By an elderly skier called Lloyd
His peculiar stance

Caused a huge avalanche
So his lift pass was made null and void

Nigel Lloyd, whose snowploughs were chronic,
Skied well after one gin and tonic,
But after a few
His skis fairly flew
As his speed entered realms supersonic

Although she found Verbier pretty
Judy longed to ski Mexico City
But sad to relate
It's not snowed there to date
Which is really a terrible pity

An over-weight lady called Nina
Claimed she'd ski like a snow ballerina
But in mid pirouette
She lost her brave bet
And fell down a hole in Cortina

After skiing 10 thousand resorts
Arnie wrote a whole book of reports
When he finally faltered
Nine thousand had altered
So all his research came to naught

*A keen office worker called Grundy
Disappeared skiing home late one Monday
Then, watching TV
Mrs G cried with glee
"Look it's Dad – he's come 12th on Ski Sunday!"

On being appointed PR for a Lacrosse team
  Said Michael "My job's just the ticket
  But is it remotely like cricket?
  I've just no idea
  How the game's played I fear
  Do I catch it or hit it or kick it?

It was claimed the Nazis thought cricket was a secret British method of training the elite classes to throw hand grenades – and had we played them at cricket the war might have ended sooner.
  *The Third Reich were 13 for 9
  When Adolf came in, screaming: "Schwein!"*
  Then he stamped violently
  "Your grenades don't fool me!"
  But was blasted to bits by a mine.

  Said a much reformed batsman called Botham
  "I'm back and I'll bloody well show them!"
  He behaved during parties
  Drank pop and ate smarties
  And smoked herbal fags till he loathed them

  *In the Beasties and Bugs game of cricket
  The cockroach was caught trying to snick it
  The Gnat said "Owzat!" –
  Beat the Centipede's bat
  He was out – 60 legs before wicket

  *An extremely tall oarsman called Mace
  Was Oxford's big hope in the race
  But just as they sped off
  A bridge knocked his head off
  And the dark blues were sunk without trace

Looking back at Erica Roe's celebrated Twickenham streak on Jan 2, 1982 when England played Australia and won 15-11. But who cared about the score when this happened!
A streaker called Erica Roe
Had breasts that were seen swinging low
When at Twickers she ran
One much impressed fan
Shouted loudly: "Go Erica, go!"

When my friend Steve Hartridge's football team didn't live up to expectations.
Said Stevie: "There's trouble at t'mill
My team must be over the hill
My wondrous boys Brighton
Should have shown much more fightin'
And after all that it's nil nil!"

AND:
When Steve, with a funny tin hat on
The front of a snow-cat he sat on
He advanced to the front
In a daft war-games stunt
Saying: "How do I look – just like Patton?"

Ode to a footballing barrister.
A ball-playing barrister, Patwick
Played football one Sunday for Gatwick
Trying three different wigs
He aped Ryan Giggs
And scored a most memorable hat-twick

Janice, a World Cup fanatic
On the touchline was so acrobatic
When the ball hit her head
She rang home and said:
"I've just scored for Brazil – I'm ecstatic!"

Happy memories of the 50th Monaco Grand Prix.
When some race fans at Monte on Sea
Tried to see who would win the Grand Prix
Gloria gazed at the track
And was quite taken back
Saying "Goodness – it's Willie's MG!"

Dan Dare turns 70.
"I'm old and my back-pain's infernal"
Wrote Dan in his space pilot's journal
"I've been fighting green men
Since I've no idea when -
So how come I'm still just a colonel?"

Said a reader: "Way back in my teens
I was hoping to find lady Treens
I was sure Sondar's mum
Would be pretty – not dumb
My Venus in vivid green jeans!"

Politics

Said Anthony Blair, with great glee
"Elections waste time – can't you see?
The voters are fools
So I'm changing the rules
They can only choose Cherie or me."

The Donald
The President's getting the hump
He's making his White House staff jump
Keeping aliens at bay
And grumbling all day
Now they're calling the guy Forrest Trump

Though Theresa was ready for Brexit
The stubborn old Lords almost wrecked it
The deal looked just fine –
She was ready to sign
Then the Barons and Earls blocked the exit
(But only temporarily!)

Denis Thatcher*
Gasped Denis: "My wife's won AGAIN!
She doesn't know when to say when
Will she ever retire?
She must know I'll expire ...
I'm already a hundred and ten!"

It was rumoured that Margaret Thatcher agreed her organs could be donated for transplants. If other contemporary party leaders would so the same, you could forget elections and just create the perfect party leader.

*They plucked out the heart of young Neil
Owen's ears added much sex appeal
Then with David Steel's eyes
And Maggie's lean thighs
They created Miss Thatchkin O'Steel.

When they jailed a Korean called Kim
It sounded so final and grim
But oh dearie me
He's still fancy free
It turned out it just wasn't 'im

Said a skier called Einstein: "I'm weary
Of skiing so fast that quite clearly
When I ski at such height
I must *schuss* fast as light –
But I must say it's only a theory ...!"

At Christmas mean Mr McTay
Sent his wife's birthday card from last
May
Saying: "Just a wee peep,
It's nay yours tay keep –
I'll need it for Valentine's day!"

A pilot who loved his au-pair
Towed a Valentine card through the air
But his wife spoiled his fun
With a big Ack Ack gun
And now the au pair's in despair

A time-machine captain called Vaughn
Found the future just made him forlorn
He rushed back too fast,
Hurtled back to the past
Thus arriving too soon to be born

When her pen-pal proposed to her, Betty
Hacked a path to him with a machete
But on reaching Tibet
She became most upset
For her husband to be was a Yeti

Christmas & Valentine's Day

*Our Santa complained to his reindeers
"Christmas nears, what a pain, not again dears!
This climbing down chimneys
Is SUCH a fraught bizzneys
Let's scrap the idea – it's insane dears!"

A limerick for Christmas or Valentine's Day.
*At Christmas mean Mr McTay
Sent his wife's birthday card from last May
Saying: "Just a wee peep,
It's nay yours tay keep –
I'll need it for Valentine's day!"

On post-Christmas diets.
*To diminish his festive spare tyres
Mr Meyers clamped his jaw with strong wires
So severe was his fast
That he soon breathed his last …
Mrs Meyers had hidden the pliers

*A pilot who loved his au-pair
Towed a Valentine card through the air
But his wife spoiled his fun
With a big Ack Ack gun
And now the au pair's in despair

Timeless

*When her pen-pal proposed to her, Betty
Hacked a path to him with a machete
But on reaching Tibet
She became most upset
For her husband to be was a Yeti

*How do we men lose individual socks so easily? Apparently
they can get sucked – under great force – through the drain-
pipe filter and are literally washed away... presumably out
to sea!*
"The foot I'm on pongs" said the sock
To a brassiere, a vest and a frock
So it squeezed out unseen
From the washing machine
To be drowned in East India Dock

*When a crime-fiction writer called Barr
Met his end it was somewhat bizarre
As he finished the plot
He was suddenly shot
"The killer" he typed "is called ... ARRRGGGHHH!!!"

*A Frenchman called Monsieur le Bone
Tried to tunnel to England alone.
He completely missed Dover
Skirted Omsk and Bolsover
And popped up in Sierra Leone

Following the first documented suicide by an industrial robot:
*A car factory robot called Piers
Went berserk when he tried a few beers
He dismantled his Mum
Melted down a close chum
And welded Big Ends to his ears

*A gormless young spy from Dalkeith
Bit his girlfriend to death on the heath
The passionate Scot
Had completely forgot
He'd put cyanide pills in his teeth

On Gerald Ratner's "crap" PR disaster.
*A smash and grab burglar called Smee
Raided Ratners at Sarfend-on-Sea
He snatched 50 rings
Some tiaras and fings
But 'is 'aul was worf just 90 pee!

*During Sports Day, a very large nun
Huffed and puffed in her convent's Fun Run
But her bountiful shape
Meant she breasted the tape
The instant the race had begun

*When a boozy young mother called Julia
Fed her babies, they went all peculiar.
One breast dispensed gin
To her thirstier twin
While the other was rather Drambuier

34

Space – the final frontier

*A time-machine captain called Vaughn
Found the future just made him forlorn
He rushed back too fast,
Hurtled back to the past
Thus arriving too soon to be born

The Pope indicated that his televised blessings were only valid if received "live" – even if beamed via satellite from outer space.
*When the Pope gave a blessing from space
The boffins were all in disgrace.
He was launched the wrong way
So his words went astray
And converted the whole Martian race

Another, similar, but the archbishop of Canterbury this time:
*In a satellite blessing, His Grace
Was mistakenly launched into space.
After preaching from Mars
He sped on to the stars
While the whole general synod gave chase

*In the middle of something ecstatic
Two astronauts grunted "Oh drat it!"
They'd been blown into space
By a violent embrace –
Some nights you can still see 'em at it!

35

And still in space (a favourite topic!)
*An astronomer shouted "Ah HA!
I've spotted a fearsome death star
But it's light years away
So we'll all be OK
It can't possibly travel this fa ... aaarrrggghhh!"

*On his way to the nuclear summit
Mr Gorbachev glimpsed Halley's Comet
Suspecting a missile,
He said with a hiss: "I'll
Send orders to Moscow to bomb it!"

*An astronomer royal called Gromett
Thought he'd stumbled across a new comet
But going outside
His telescope spied
That a seagull had whoopsied upon it

RIP Sir Patrick Moore. I wrote this before his death and imagined him exploding at the BBC! Of course it didn't happen that way when the poor chap did die.
*Said Sir Patrick, aglow on the screen
"I'm expanding – a riveting scene!
My time here is over
I've gone supernova!"...
Up in smoke went the Beeb's new canteen

*A Martian grew one extra head
"I'm a freak – I'll destroy us" he said
But being a dunce
Only hanged himself once ...
So the poor chap's by no means all dead

36

When a newspaperman found a way
Of travelling through time he'd say: "Hey!
Here's my very first mission – read tomorrow's edition
"Then come back and write it today!"

China enters the space race
  *An 18-stone spaceman called Choo
Kept losing the rest of his crew.
While they floated weightless
He said "Wish I ate less"
In space he still weighed 9 stone two

*In the Martian political poll
The Greens have just taken control
The Bug-Eyed Blue Giants
Split the Flat Mars Alliance
Now the Prime Minister's heads will all roll

"Captain, come quickly!" said Spock
"An alien craft's trying to dock!"
But beamed up by Scottie
Kirk yelled (with bare botty)
"I was just in the bath ya daft jock!"

Apparently British cosmonaut Helen Sharman grew by an inch during her Soviet space mission in 1991. Could this be a chance for those of reduced stature to achieve similar results? Sadly, in the case of the tiny comedian Ronnie Corbett, a secret mission to the cosmos had an unexpected effect:
  When they rocketed into the Blue
The rest of the crew grew and grew
But cosmonaut Corbett
Returning from orbit
Found he'd shrunk – and was now one foot two.

Odds & ends

On British Rail saying trains up to 10 minutes late are "on time".

Said the booking clerk: "Look, sorry mate
The next train's on time so just wait
But the 4.10 from Purley
Is four minutes early
Which could mean it's six minutes late."

A cook, in Tibet, on a climb
Said: "We've run out of herbs – it's a crime
The weather's too ghastly
To find much wild parsley
So I may be outside for some thyme!"

An expert on fossils called Steiger
Found some interesting bones near the Niger
Not, alas, ancient man
But his loving wife Jan
Who'd been eaten that night by a tiger

A punctual young lady called Gwen
Had delusions of time now and then
She'd cry "I'm a clock
Hear my tick. And my tock!"
Now she often stands in for Big Ben!

Scientists have worked out the maximum weight for a land mammal. Anything more than 100 tons would (a) be unable to move, and b) if it could move would break all its legs.

The most gross dinosaur in creation
Found himself in a sad situation
If he tried chasing prey
All his legs would give way
So he stood there and died of starvation.

An expert in much-flattened fauna
Said: "There's something I dread round the corner ..."
He was right – 'twas no rat
Nor a careless young cat
But the corpse of his doting Aunt Lorna

An ambitious young woman called Cara
Felt her status should rise much much far-er
She ignored hoi polloi
But had little joy
As she couldn't afford a tiara

A student of humour called Garth
Tried to work out what made people laugh
He found taking the piss
Was all hit and miss
And would just fall asleep in his bath

When an MBA scholar called Gina
Found herself in the job-hunt arena
She was quickly in luck
And earned mega-bucks
With a fabulous job as a cleaner

A randy young writer from Beddingham
Snogged women no sooner than gedding them
Though keener than mustard
And much as he lusted
He'd always stop short of a'wedding'em

Screamed the Ed, in a bit of a rage
"How d'you expect to be earning a wage
Your copy is LATE ...
Past its new sell by date ...
We're about to dispense with your page."

A stunning young lady call Lill
Had looks that could instantly kill
In fact so many died
That the girl, full of pride,
Was eventually jailed by the Bill

When she found she'd become a myope
A typist called Rose had an eye-op
But it made her no better
When she typed out a letter
It always come out as "qwertyuiop"

Riksgränsen, northern Sweden on mid-summer's day.
Said an owl in a North Arctic zoo
"I'm confused – don't know what I should do.
When it's daytime all night
I'm no longer a fright
So it's pointless to shriek 'tu-whit tu-whoo!'"

A priest spent a week and half
Hiding under the Vatican bath
Then filmed the nude Pope
As he reached for the soap
Yelling: "Now to il banco I laugh!"

When trying to ape Wordsworth or Goethe
A Canadian suffered inertia
Saying: "Had they lived here
"They'd have had a lean year
"There's not one bloomin' daff in Alberta!"

Sometimes hard to find Indian Tonic water in India!
Said our Indian guide "It's ironic
You can get upset tums and bubonic
You'll get hab-dabs all right
But try as you might
You can't get an Indian tonic!"

On his birthday a chap called O'Grady
Went to France for the day with his lady
But the two-timing skunk
Got incredibly drunk
And canoodled with someone called Sadie.

When a bubbly lady in York
Had a visit one night from a stork
The resulting young lad
Was just like his Dad
Chasing girls long before he could talk

A watch-mending poet called Hall
Wrote his verses incredibly small
His watchmaker's glass
Caused the problem, alas
For no-one could read them at all

Predictable Joe, for his starter
Had plateloads of stuffed Green tomater
But Arnie, dull lad
Was almost as bad
With endless Tara-masalater

Said a pedant: "They're wrong and I'm right
When it's dark I'll insist that it's light
The sky isn't blue
One and one isn't two
And I'm sorry but black's really white!"

An unfortunate chappie called Hess
Said: "40 years on, I'm a mess.
I've not fed the cat
Or tidied my flat
And my lav's in a hell of a mess!"

*In September 2017 my good friend and fellow former Fleet
Street reporter Frank "Scoop" Baldwin turned 60, prompt-
ing the following limerick.*
Said Scoop, quite a prince of reporters
"I'm 59 now – and four quarters.
But as onwards I soldier
I become far less older
Than the ages – combined – of my daughters!"

A rare double limerick:
The (now) late clairvoyant Doris Stokes reported that (the late) Diana Dors was cross with her (equally late) husband, Alan Lake.

A spiritual lady called Stokes
Sends us gossip of heavenly folks
Of Marilyn Monroe
Dating Jack's father Joe
And of Rock seeing all kinds of blokes.
While there's no word of old Steve McQueen
Mrs Pankhurst's in love with James Dean
And that Ernest Marples
Has wed Ena Sharples
While Albert's two-timing his Queen.

Royalty

This was written in 1985 before the death of Wallis Simpson. (If Edward VII hadn't abdicated, she could in theory have been queen until his death in 1972.)
  Mrs Simpson has long been our Queen
  And many things haven't yet been
  George the 6th isn't yet
  They've not crowned Lillibet
  And the QAE2's yet to be seen

  *Prince Philip saw Charles and said: "Heck!!
  What's that collar you've got round your neck?"
  Said Charles with a sob:
  "One's been given a job –
  I'm the Rev at All Souls, Tooting Bec!"

  *Said Prince Philip: "Chinese? They're a menace
  Keep asking how big Number 10 is.
  And on the Great Wall
  They had the sheer gall
  To say to me: 'You must be Denis!'"

Prince Charles' love affair with plants.
  *While chatting to lupins of late
  Prince Charlie got into a state
  A shrivelled-up rose
  Said: "I don't dare suppose
  You could bloody well water me mate?"

44

On the opening of Terminal 4 (1986).
  *Since Charles opened Terminal 4
  Life at Windsor's been one endless roar
  When the Queen sends for kippers
  Or Prince Philip's slippers
  She's now forced to use semaphore

When Charles injured his arm.
  *The hand of our yet-to-be king
  Is healing, the clumsy old thing
  He said: "The pain lingers
  When I use all the fingers …
  It's so hard to scratch with a sling."

The Royal Family may sometimes seem a little like soap characters – it could become increasingly difficult to tell them apart!
  *Dirty Den – News at Ten – has the gen:
  Roland Rat's new address: Number 10
  Prince Andrew's in Dallas
  And Joan runs the Palace
  While the Queen reads the News now and then

On the Queen's tour of China.
  *The Queen tackled sweet-and-sour pork
  With chopsticks which stabbed like a hawk,
  But when the Chow Mein
  Trickled down the royal chin
  She grabbed for a large spoon and fork

The Queen's birthday.
  *Said Liz: "Being Queen is such fun
  That One feels One has scarcely begun
  D'You think Charles will mind
  If one hasn't resigned
  Until One's one hundred and one?"

The Queen revealed she enjoys listening to Radio 2 announcers Ken Bruce and the late Derek Jameson.
  *Said the Queen: "One enjoys hearing Ken
  Even Jameson is fun now and then
  But too much exposure
  To 'im really throws yer –
  Oi may never talk proper again!"

Prince Andrew and Fergie's honeymoon.
  *A postcard from distant Azores
  Has been sent to dear Fergie's in-laws
  Saying "Wonderful trip
  But not enough kip …
  Didn't warn me how loud Andy snores!"

  (Now it's over, it has to be said
  'twas not Andy and Fergie who wed
  To avoid any trouble
  Each one used a double
  They married LAST Wednesday instead)

Plain daft

It emerged that you could see the Urals from the top of the Hoover building in west London.
  *A Hoover employee called Geek
  Tried to peep at a Soviet peak
  But he looked the wrong way
  And in Labrador Bay
  Saw an Eskimo having a leak.

  *A jilted young vet from Glencoe
  Sent an un-Valentine to her beau
  It released several fleas
  Sprayed manure on his knees
  And a horse-shoe destroyed his big toe

Fears of countryside being affected by radiation after Chernobyl.
  *Mary's suffered a serious blow
  Her pet lamb will just have to go
  For wherever she gads
  She's forced to count Rads
  And her poor little lamb's sure to glow.

  When a hooker at Blackpool on Sea
  Tried to visit a Tory MP
  The police said "Alas
  Since you haven't a pass
  You can't enter – and neither can he!"
(Banned by the Daily Star 1985, during Conservative Party Conference.)

47

After hearing that a female chimp's backside apparently expands when she feels romantic:
*On the phone to his girl, shouted Gus:
"Hurry home, Dad's gone out – it's just us"
But her bottom expanded –
She found herself stranded
On top of a No 4 bus.

*A dictionary writer called Fred
Had a breakdown upon reaching Z
After Zonda and Zho
Zip, Zeph and Zygo
He shouted and stood on his head

*A choirboy whose mum said: "Don't mutter, Kit"
Sang a carol but frequently st-stuttered it.
It t-took him s-so long
To f-finish his s-song
It was springtime before he had ut-uttered it.

When Peter Tory's Sunday Express *column (along with my limericks) was axed by Eve Pollard:*
*"I'm sorry" said Eve, "but this ditty
Is really not terribly witty.
Unlike Edward Lear,
You have no career
As a poet my dear, what a pity!"

*Two tramps who got sloshed on Nouveau
Said: "The bouquet smellsh jusht like B.O.
Itsh corked for a shtart
And hopeleshly tart …
Lasht yearsh wash much more – *comme il faut!*"

My family & friends

Looking back at my twin daughters Amber and Lara on their 28th birthday.
When Amber arrived, one of two
She grew and she grew and she grew
She's 28 now
Much taller – and how – than she was back in 72

When little, our wonderful La
Left the door of our Volvo ajar
She's 28 now
Still with us, somehow
Even though she fell out of the car! (*True!*)

For my (now 21-year-old) grandson Oliver Spalding on his (then) 3rd birthday.
On his birthday, a young man called Ollie
Got a lousy old T-shirt – what folly!
"What's this load of tat?"
Asked the ungrateful brat ...
"I'd much rather just have the lolly!"

For my former mother-in-law, Rowena (Marli) MacDonald Watson from genteel Ardleigh, Essex.
There was a young lady called Marli
Who went on a Kenyan safari
Between shooting cheetahs
She drank several litres
Of Campari ('ardly the done thing in Ardleigh)

Marli's birthday 1986.
While taking a fortnight's Swiss vac
Mrs Mac toppled into Le Lac
It was really quite fun
But the damage was done
And all she can say now is QUACK!

Commiserating with my Swedish sister-in-law and brother-in-law on holiday in Scotland.
Said Tommy to Ammy in Skye
"The rain will stop soon, by and by"
But it didn't, you know
So they just had to go
And went back to Sweden and cried

For a Breckenridge, Colorado (friends') dog nicknamed "The Nerd".
Said the Nerd to the bird: "How absurd!
"You're just feathered while I'm richly furred ..."
Said the bird: "Tweetie-pie
That's why I can fly –
So at least I don't step in my turd!"

My old TV chum, Stuart.
Said a cameraman, Stu, with some feeling
"Fings just ain't the same now since Ealing
Wot wiv digital crap
And plots that are pap
Today's films just ain't so appealing!"

My pal Jeremy Ashpool, boss of Jeremy's, my favourite restaurant (in Haywards Heath).
When Jeremy skied the Inferno
His wife said: "My goodness – Ooh er no!"
But just like Jean-Claude
He would surely have soared
If he'd not stopped en route for a Pernod

Jeremy's Danish wife, Vera.
Said birthday girl Vera: "Let's dine!
"I'm 60 – let's have some more wine!"
Then declared: "For god's sake
I've made a mistake ...
I've realised I'm just 59!"

Vera's husband again – alias "Jezza".
"It's Vera's big day!" shouted Jezza
"Bring Champagne!" and a waiter said "Yessir!"
"Just a tumbler or two,
For each one of you?
Or maybe a Nebuchadnezzar?"

My former GP Bruce Lambert.
An athletic young doctor called Bruce
Used to dose himself up with strong juice
Till he thought he could fly
As high in the sky
As a frisky young Canada goose!

Challenged by my Spanish chum Leo to write a limerick about Prosecco, I got side-tracked and came up with this:
When a fat voyeuristic young gecko
Heard a really mysterious echo
He discovered two lovers
Beneath the bed covers
And pleaded "ooh do let me have a quick decko!"

Another Leo challenge – write one about Hanneke. Rhyming is not the problem – it's the rhythm – and whether the lines scan! Sometimes a difficult word can make it more fun.
Said a lovely young lady called Hanneke
"People WILL keep on calling me Annika …
The fact that I'm Dutch
Doesn't bother them much
And at least they don't call me Britannica!"

More about Leo himself.
When Leo moved house back to Spain
There was nothing but wind, floods and rain
He said "Where's Noah's ark?
Sod this for a lark"
And moved back to Sussex again.

Although he knew nothing of cricket
When Leo advanced down the wicket
He terrified all
Without bowling a ball
They all fled for naught – just the ticket!

Said Leo "I'm taking no chances"
As he endlessly toured Spanish ranches
In the hope that he'd find
A bull that was blind
And thus wouldn't see his sharp lances

When my Fleet Street pal Peter Hardy was (bizarrely)
offered a job as a Tesco delivery driver.
When an ex-war reporter called Pete
Ran a Tesco delivery fleet
He risked certain jail
As he would, without fail,
Keep a gun on the passenger seat

When Peter and his wife Felice holidayed in Westendorf
near Kitzbühel, Austria with their dog Jackson ...
On a sweltering walk around Kitzbühel
Jackson sweated – it wasn't a bit cool
Red hot like a heater,
He growled and bit Peter
Thank goodness he wasn't a pit bull

And news of their (now sadly departed) Jack Russell, Spot.
When Spot reached a hundred and five
He exclaimed "and now I shall strive
To add further years
To my lifetime, my dears
But it's wonderful I'm still alive!"

A rampaging Spaniard, no less
Was rather enamoured of Tess
"Do you fancy me lass?"
He asked – made a pass
And her answer was quick – she screamed YES!!!!!

Two look-alike chums, who love pretending to be each other!
(Luckily Rob, like Peter James, doesn't mind being insulted.)
 A funny old pair, Frank and Rob
 Alike as two peas in a pod
 But while Frank smiles a bit
 That Rob, the old git
 Is an utterly miserable sod

And I got this reply from Frank – the "smiley" one!
 Said Frank: "No objections from me
 But you can't use my name for free!
 T'would be so much better
 To send me a letter
 Enclosing my usual fee!"

One written specially for my publishers!
 A biographer based in Rwanda
 Wanted background about Hastings Banda
 But en route to Malawi
 On the back of his Harley
 He got lost and turned up in Uganda

For my Danish dentist friends.
 If you get a bad tooth now and then ...
 And there really is no knowing when.
 If you can't stand the pain
 Just send for a Dane
 You simply can't beat Mads or Sven

 When a peaceful young writer called Dacre
 Was felled by a colleague's haymaker
 He said with a glare
 "That was rather unfair!
 But I won't hit you back – I'm a Quaker!"

Said a poet "I'm having weird dreams
About squid, giant prawns and sardines
That fill fishing boats
So I make lots of notes
And convert them to Alexandrines."

And (carpenter/builder) Tommy's 60th birthday.
Said Tommy, "It's tough getting older
As a young man I really was bolder
No longer a hippy
I'm now just a chippy
Whose knees start to knock when it's colder."

*From my ski magazine editing days – our main ski writer
skied anything that moved – volcanoes, icebergs, you
name it.*
A foolish young man called Andreas
Skied such dangerous peaks it was chaos
Till an iceberg devoured him
And quite overpowered him
What a pity he'd never obey us!

An entrepreneur, name of Luscombe
For whom selling firms was the custom
Had glowing remarks
On so many plaques
That he struggled to find time to dust'em

On his very first trip to Zermatt
Henry gasped in surprise in mid-chat
The Matterhorn rock
Gave him quite a big shock,
And he yelled: "What the bloody hell's that?"

My (slim) wife Vivianne's unnecessary attempts to diet. (I got plenty of nuffin!)
  Said Vivianne, huffin' and puffin'
  "I've got to get rid of my muffin!"
  She went without dinner,
  Got thinner and thinner,
  And finally, folks, there was nuffin'!

And this about Vivianne too:
  When a dishy young girl, Vivianne
  Sunbathed naked all weekend in Cannes
  The men formed a queue
  To admire such a view
  And by golly, she got such a tan

For my good friend Neil English
  When a charming young chappie called Neil
  Developed an odd flower appeal
  He ate tons of roses
  And various posies
  But longed for a decent square meal

My friend Bryan Hirst.
  Said Hirsty: "It just isn't fair!
  I'm broke and the cupboard is bare!
  Let's start a new flight
  To Ryde, Isle of Wight –
  And christen the thing Bryan Air!"

Major General Sir Frank Richardson, war hero, honorary surgeon to the Queen and bagpipe competition judge (who listened without his hearing aid) – and wrote books about gay generals.

A bagpipe judge, deaf in one ear
Reckoned lots our generals were queer
And Flo of the Lamp
Was seriously camp
No wonder she hated Crimea